A TASTE OF FJB

A COLLECTION OF RECIPES FOR SWEETS SERVED

AT THE FRIENDS OF JUPITER BEACH MONTHLY

BEACH CLEANUPS

www.friendsofjupiterbeach.org

Written By: Mark Holbert & Joan Ross

A TASTE OF FJB

Contents

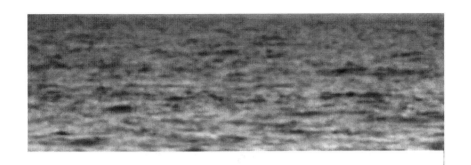

ABOUT FJB

A MESSAGE FROM THE PRESIDENT

The Friends of Jupiter Beach or FJB, started in 1994 with about 30 concerned people who loved the beach. Today we are over 5,000 individuals, families and businesses. Since the beginning, we have been supported by hundreds of donations from local people who use our beach as well as from people all over the country who have visited Jupiter and send us letters and donations thanking us for this special beach. We have never received public funding, yet we would, however, like to express our appreciation to the officials and the employees of the Town of Jupiter who make it possible for us to contribute and function happily in this beautiful Town. We would like to thank the many members of the Press & Media who have helped us along the way. We have done our best to give back to this community by caring for our beach.

Our volunteers have cleaned Jupiter Beach on the first Saturday of each month since November 1994. We used to think we were doing very well if 15 of us showed up. Today, 150-250 of us show up! Today our schools are participating and we are teaching young people good citizenship by our example and their involvement. Today, local businesses and individuals are helping this effort with generous and enthusiastic support, making it possible for us to serve a beautiful breakfast at Ocean Cay Park following each cleanup. Today, we donate over 400,000 bags a year to keep our dog boxes along the beach filled.

We patrol the beach; offer Community Service hours to those who wish them; reach out to the Community and work with other like-spirited organizations. Today, the Solid Waste Authority recognizes us as their OFFICIAL Adopt-A-Spot group of this stretch of Jupiter Beach.

Since, we have started keeping track of our measurements, we calculate that we have removed over 74,000 pounds of garbage and saved over $500,000 in taxpayer dollars by our cleanup efforts. In addition, the benefit of having clean beaches goes beyond the environmental aspect. Individuals travel from inside and outside of the county each weekend with their furry family members. They eat in our amazing restaurants, shop in our stores, and stay in our wonderful hotels. Many people have said one of the reasons they have moved to Jupiter is because of the dog friendly beaches.

This book is dedicated to all the wonderful volunteers that have helped and continue to help Friends of Jupiter Beach throughout the years. Without the support of these individuals, our beaches would just be another beach.

We hope that you enjoy the recipes in the book just as much as we have on the first Saturday of every month for the past many years. We encourage you to come out to our monthly cleanups and help us keep Jupiter's beaches "Clean and Dog Friendly".

WELCOME FROM JOAN ROSS

This recipe collection is dedicated to the many friends of Jupiter Beach who join us on the first Saturday of every to give their time and effort to clean Jupiter's beaches. Without you, our beautiful

resource would not be the treasure that is.

I am often asked for recipes for the treats I prepare for the breakfast following the cleanups. Each of the recipes in this collection has been served at one time or another cleanup over the past many years. Hopefully, your favorite is included. Most of the recipes are from "scratch", but some use mixes, and are quick and easy.

There is one very important rule when baking in South Florida. Your baking soda and baking powder must be very fresh, meaning, not more than three months old. When I purchased new baking powder and soda, I write the replacement date directly on the container, and when that day comes, out it goes. For accurate measures, please remember to aerate the flour before lightly spinning it into the measuring cup. Then level it off with the flat edge of a knife.

I know you enjoy making these recipes, and I look forward to seeing you the first Saturday of every month with more treats to try.

Bon appétit,

Joan Ross

BREADS

BANANA WALNUT BREAD

INGREDIENTS

- 2 cups flour
- ¾ teaspoon baking soda
- ½ teaspoon salt
- 1 cup sugar
- ⅓ cup butter, softened
- two large eggs
- 1 ½ cups mashed ripe bananas (about 3 large)
- ⅓ cup plain yogurt
- 1 teaspoon vanilla extract
- 1 cup walnuts

DIRECTIONS

1. Preheat oven to 350°. Coat an 8.5 x 4.5 loaf pan with baking spray. Combine flour, baking soda, and salt, stirring with a whisk.

2. Place butter and sugar in a large mixing bowl and beat with the mixer at medium speed until well blended (about one minute).

3. Add eggs, one at a time, beating well after each addition.

4. Add bananas, yogurt and vanilla, beat until blended.

5. Add flour mixture, beat on low speed until just moist. Fold in walnuts.

6. Spoon batter into prepared loaf pan and bake for 55 to 60 minutes or until tester comes out clean. Cool 10 minutes in pan on wire rack; remove from pan and cool completely.

BEST BANANA BREAD

INGREDIENTS

- Nonstick vegetable oil spray

- 1½ cups all-purpose flour

- 1¼ teaspoons baking soda

- ¾ teaspoon kosher salt

- 1 cup (packed) dark brown sugar

- ⅓ cup mascarpone, plain whole-milk Greek yogurt, or sour cream

- ¼ cup (½ stick) unsalted butter, room temperature

- 2 large eggs

- 4 large very ripe bananas, mashed (about 1½ cups)

- ½ cup chopped bittersweet or semisweet chocolate (optional)

- ½ cup chopped walnut (optional)

DIRECTIONS

1. Preheat oven to 350°. Lightly coat 8 ½ x4 ½" loaf pan with nonstick spray and line with parchment paper, leaving a generous overhang on long sides. Whisk flour, baking soda, and salt in a medium bowl.

2. Using an electric mixer on medium-high speed, beat brown sugar, mascarpone, and butter in a large bowl until light and fluffy, about 4 minutes. Add eggs one at a time, beating to blend after each addition and scraping down sides and bottom of bowl as needed.

3. Reduce speed to low, add flour mixture, and mix until just combined. Add bananas and mix just until combined. Fold in chocolate and/or walnuts, if using. Scrape batter into prepared pan; smooth top.

4. Bake bread until a tester inserted into the center comes out clean, about 40-45 minutes. Transfer pan to a wire rack and let bread cool in pan 1 hour. Turn out bread and let cool completely (if you can resist) before slicing.

BANANAS FOSTER BANANA BREAD

INGREDIENTS

Bread

- 2 cups all-purpose flour

- 1 teaspoon baking soda

- ½ teaspoon baking powder

- 1 cup granulated sugar

- ½ cup vegetable oil

- 2 eggs

- 3 medium bananas, mashed

- 1 teaspoon vanilla extract

- 3 tablespoons milk

Streusel Topping

- 1½ cups chopped walnuts

- ⅓ cup all-purpose flour

- ¼ cup dark brown sugar

- ½ teaspoon ground cinnamon

- 4 tablespoons butter

For the Rum Glaze

- ¼ cup (4 tablespoons) butter

- 2 tablespoons water

- ¼ cup light brown sugar

- ¼ cup rum

DIRECTIONS

1. Preheat oven to 350°F. Grease a 9x5-inch loaf pan.

2. Combine ingredients for streusel topping in a medium bowl and combine with fingers to create a crumbly topping with the butter evenly distributed. Set aside.

3. Whisk the flour, baking soda, and baking powder in a small bowl to combine. Set aside.

4. On medium speed, beat the sugar and vegetable oil to combine. Add the eggs, one at a time, beating after each until combined. Add the mashed bananas and vanilla extract; beat to combine. Alternatively add the flour mixture and milk, beginning and ending with the flour. Beat just until the flour is incorporated and finish mixing with a spatula.

5. Spread batter into the prepared loaf pan. Sprinkle the streusel topping evenly over the batter. Bake until a thin knife inserted in the center comes out almost clean, about 60 minutes.

6. To make the rum glaze, combine the butter, water and sugar in a saucepan over medium-high heat and bring to a boil. Immediately reduce the heat to medium-low and simmer for 5 minutes. Remove from the heat and stir in the rum. Set aside and cover to keep warm.

7. Cool the cake on a wire rack for 5 minutes. Then, using a skewer poke holes all over the top of the loaf. Spoon about ¼ cup of the rum glaze all over the loaf. Let the cake sit for about 5 minutes and then spoon the remaining glaze over it, a little at a time, until it is all absorbed into the bread.

CARROT-WALNUT LOAF CAKE

INGREDIENTS

- 1 cup vegetable oil, plus more
- 1¼ cups plus 1 tablespoon all-purpose flour; plus more
- 1½ teaspoons baking powder
- 1½ teaspoons ground cinnamon
- ½ teaspoon kosher salt
- ½ cup golden raisins
- ½ cup walnuts, coarsely chopped
- 3 large eggs
- 1 cup granulated sugar
- 2 teaspoons vanilla extract
- 8 ounces carrots, coarsely grated (about 2 cups)
- 2 teaspoons light brown sugar

DIRECTIONS

1. Preheat oven to 350°. lightly oil and flour a 9x5" loaf pan. Whisk baking powder, cinnamon, salt, and 1 ¼ cups flour

in a small bowl. Toss raisins, walnuts, and remaining 1 Tbsp. flour in another bowl.

2. Using an electric mixer on medium-high speed, beat eggs and granulated sugar in a medium bowl until light and fluffy, about 4 minutes. With mixer running, gradually drizzle in 1 cup oil, then add vanilla. Fold in dry ingredients, raisin mixture, and carrots; scrape batter into prepared pan. Sprinkle with brown sugar.

3. Bake cake until a tester inserted into the center comes out clean, about 55 minutes. Let cool slightly in pan, then turn out onto a wire rack to cool completely.

Can be made ahead: Bake up to 2 days ahead. Store wrapped at room temperature.

CHOCOLATE ZUCCHINI BANANA BREAD

INGREDIENTS

- ½ cup (40g) dark chocolate cocoa
- 1 ½ cups (180g) all-purpose flour
- 1 teaspoon baking soda
- ½ teaspoon baking powder
- ¼ teaspoon salt
- ½ teaspoon cinnamon
- ½ cup (125ml) vegetable oil
- ½ cup (100g) granulated white sugar
- ½ cup (110g) Light brown sugar, packed
- 2 large eggs
- 1 teaspoon vanilla extract
- 2 cups shredded zucchini (approximately 300g or two medium zucchinis, patted dry)

- ¾ cup mashed ripe bananas (approximately 175g about two medium bananas)

- 1 cup (175g) chocolate chips

INSTRUCTIONS

1. Preheat oven to 350° F. Spray a 5x9 loaf pan with non-stick spray, set aside.

2. In a medium mixing bowl, whisk together cocoa, flour, baking soda, baking powder, salt and cinnamon. Set aside.

3. In a large mixing bowl, mix together oil, vanilla and both sugars. Stir in eggs, bananas and shredded zucchini. Stir until well combined.

4. Fold in dry ingredients just until combined. Fold in chocolate chips. Pour batter into prepared loaf pan and bake in preheated oven for 45 to 60 minutes until a toothpick comes out clean with a few moist crumbs sticking to the toothpick.

5. Remove from oven and let cool completely. Slice and serve. Store covered at room temperature.

COCONUT BREAD

INGREDIENTS

- 4 cups sweetened coconut (10 ounces)

- 2 cups flour

- 3 teaspoons baking powder

- ½ teaspoon salt

- ½ cup unsalted butter, softened

- 1 cup sugar

- 2 large eggs

- 1 teaspoon vanilla

- 1 cup water

DIRECTIONS

1. Preheat oven to 350°. Butter and flour a 9 x 5 loaf.

2. Spread 3 cups coconut in a large shallow pan, toasting oven, stirring occasionally until evenly about 20 to 25 minutes. Watch carefully, edges burn quickly. Cool

completely then grind in a food processor into a course meal.

3. Stir together the flour, baking powder, salt and remaining cup of on toasted coconut.

4. In a large bowl, beat together butter and sugar with electric mixer about 1 to 2 minutes.

5. Add eggs one at a time, beating well after each addition. Whisk 1 cup water into flour mixture, then add egg mixture until well blended.

6. Pour into loaf pan, smoothing top, and bake about 50 to 60 minutes, until tester comes out clean. Cool bread in pan on wire rack for 10 minutes, then turn out of pan. Cool completely.

DUTCH APPLE WALNUT BREAD

INGREDIENTS

TOPPING

- ¼ cup sugar

- ¼ cup flour

- 2 teaspoons cinnamon

- ¼ cup (½ stick) cold butter, cut into ½-inch pieces

In a medium bowl, whisk together the sugar, flour and cinnamon. Cut in the cold butter until the mixture becomes crumbly. Set aside.

BREAD

- ½ cup (1 stick) butter, softened 1 cup sugar

- 2 eggs

- ¼ cup plus 1 tablespoon buttermilk

- 1 teaspoon vanilla

- 2 cups (8.5 ounces) flour 1 teaspoon baking soda ½ teaspoon salt

- 2 cups peeled and diced apples
- ½ cup chopped walnuts
- Prepared topping

DIRECTIONS

1. Heat the oven to 350 degrees. Grease a 9 x 5 x 3-inch baking dish. Line the base of the dish with parchment paper, then grease the top of the parchment paper.

2. In the bowl of a stand mixer, or in a large bowl using an electric mixer, cream together the butter and sugar until light and fluffy, 3 to 5 minutes. Add the eggs, one at a time, beating well until fully incorporated. Beat in the buttermilk and vanilla.

3. In a medium bowl, whisk together the flour, baking soda and salt. With the mixer running, slowly beat in the dry ingredients just until fully combined. Stir in the diced apples and chopped walnuts by hand.

4. Pour the batter into the prepared dish, then sprinkle over the topping.

5. Place the dish in the oven and bake until puffed and a toothpick inserted comes out clean, about 55 minutes to an hour. Cool the dish on a rack for 15 minutes, then unmold and cool completely before slicing.

HONEY PUMPKIN BREAD

INGREDIENTS

- ⅔ cups granulated sugar, plus 2 tablespoons for topping
- 1 teaspoon ground cinnamon
- 1 ⅔ cups all-purpose flour
- ½ teaspoon ground nutmeg
- ½ teaspoon ground cloves
- ¾ teaspoon baking soda
- ¼ teaspoon salt
- 3 large eggs, room temperature
- ⅔ cups vegetable oil
- ⅓ cup honey
- ½ teaspoon lemon extract
- 2 teaspoons vanilla extract
- 1 cup pure pumpkin puree

DIRECTIONS

1. Preheat the oven to 350 degrees F. Grease and flour a 9x5" loaf pan (or use parchment paper).

2. In a large bowl, mix together the flour, ⅔ cups sugar, cinnamon, nutmeg, cloves, baking soda, and salt together.

3. In a medium bowl, mix together all the wet ingredients and whisk well. until well-combined.

4. Add the wet ingredients to the dry ingredients and mix until it is combined and there are no streaks of flour.

5. Pour the batter into the loaf pan and spread evenly. Sprinkle the top with the two tablespoons of sugar.

6. Bake for about 45-50 minutes, or until a toothpick comes out with a few crumbs clinging to the toothpick.

7. Remove and allow to cool completely.

LEMON BLUEBERRY BREAD

INGREDIENTS

- 2 cups flour
- ⅔ cup +1 tablespoon sugar
- 1 teaspoon baking powder
- 1 teaspoon baking soda
- ½ teaspoon salt
- 8 ounces lemon yogurt
- ¼ cup butter, melted
- one egg, lightly beaten
- 2 teaspoon grated lemon peel
- 1 teaspoon vanilla extract
- 2 cups fresh or frozen, drained frozen blueberries

DIRECTIONS

1. Preheat oven to 350°.

2. In a large bowl, stir together flour, ⅔ cup of sugar, powder, baking soda, and salt.

3. In another bowl, combine until blended yogurt, butter, egg, lemon peel and vanilla.

4. Making well in the center of dry ingredients and add yogurt mixture; stir to just combine. Stir in the blue berries.

5. Turn batter into a 9 x 5 loaf pan, sprayed with baking spray. Sprinkle with remaining 1 tablespoon sugar.

6. Bake for 45 minutes, or until a tester comes out clean.

7. Cool bread in pan on wire rack for 10 minutes, then remove from pan and cool completely.

MARBLED-CHOCOLATE BANANA

INGREDIENTS

- 2 cups flour
- ¾ teaspoon baking soda
- half teaspoon salt
- 1 cup sugar
- ¼ cup butter, softened new one and a half cups mashed ripe bananas (about 3)
- two eggs
- ⅓ cup plain yogurt
- half a cup semi-sweet chocolate chips

DIRECTIONS

1. Preheat oven to 350°. Spray a 9 x 5 loaf pan with baking spray. Combine the flour, baking soda, and salt, stirring with a whisk.

2. Place sugar and butter in a large bowl, beat with the mixer at medium speed until well blended (about 1 minute).

3. Banana, eggs, and yogurt, beat until blended. Add flour mixture, beat on low speed until just moist.

4. Place chocolate chips in a medium microwave safe bowl, and microwave at high 1 minute or until almost melted, stirring until smooth. Cool slightly.

5. Add 1 cup batter, stirring until well combined. Spoon chocolate batter alternately with plane batter into pan. Swirl batters together using a knife.

6. Bake at 350° for one hour, or until a tester inserted in the center comes out clean.

7. Cool 10 minutes in pan on wire rack, removed from pan. Cool completely.

ORANGE-CHIP CRANBERRY BREAD

INGREDIENTS

- 2 ½ cups all-purpose flour
- 1 cup sugar
- ½ teaspoon baking powder
- ½ teaspoon baking soda
- ¼ teaspoon salt
- 2 large eggs, room temperature
- ¾ cup vegetable oil
- 2 teaspoons grated orange zest
- 1 cup buttermilk
- 1 ½ cups chopped fresh or frozen cranberries, thawed
- 1 cup miniature semisweet chocolate chips
- 1 cup chopped walnuts
- ¾ cup confectioners' sugar, optional
- 2 tablespoons orange juice, optional

DIRECTIONS

1. In a bowl, combine the first 5 ingredients. In another bowl, combine eggs, oil and orange zest; mix well. Add to dry ingredients alternately with buttermilk. Fold in cranberries, chocolate chips and walnuts.

2. Pour into 2 greased 8 x 4 in. loaf pans. Bake at 350° for 45-50 minutes or until a toothpick inserted in the center comes out clean. Cool for 10 minutes before removing from pans to wire racks. If glaze is desired. combine confectioners' sugar and orange juice until smooth; spread over cooled loaves.

RHUBARB CINNAMON-NUT BREAD

INGREDIENTS

- 1 ½ cups sugar

- ½ cup finely chopped

- toasted pecans or walnuts

- 2 teaspoons cinnamon

- 2 cups flour

- 1 teaspoon baking powder

- ½ teaspoon salt

- 1 egg

- 1 cup milk

- ⅓ cup vegetable oil

- 1 cup chopped fresh or thawed frozen rhubarb

DIRECTIONS

1. Preheat oven to 350°F. Grease and flour bottom and ½ inch up sides of a 5x9-inch loaf pan.

2. Stir together ½ cup of sugar, the pecans, and cinnamon in a small bowl.

3. Stir together flour, baking powder, salt. and remaining cup sugar in a large bowl. In another bowl, beat egg with a fork; stir in milk and oil. Add egg mixture to flour mixture. Stir until just moistened (batter should be lumpy). Fold in rhubarb.

4. Spoon half of batter into prepared pan, then sprinkle with half of cinnamon mixture. Repeat with remaining batter and cinnamon mixture, using a table knife or thin metal spatula, cut down through batter and pull up in a circular motion to marble the cinnamon mixture.

5. Bake until a toothpick inserted in center comes out clean, 45-50 minutes. Transfer pan to a wire rack and let cool 10minutes. Remove bread and let cool completely on rack. Wrap with plastic wrap and let stand overnight at room temperature before slicing. (You don't have to wait overnight, but the bread is much easier to slice and has a better texture if you do. It keeps up to 3 days, wrapped and at room temperature, or frozen up to 3 months in a zip-top plastic bag.)

STRAWBERRY PINEAPPLE BREAD

INGREDIENTS

- 1 (10 ounce) package of strawberries (fresh or frozen)

- ½ (20 ounce) can crushed pineapple, drained

- 4 eggs, beaten

- 1 ¼ cups vegetable oil

- 2 cups sugar

- 3 cups all-purpose flour

- 1 teaspoon baking soda

- 1 teaspoon salt

- 2 teaspoons ground cinnamon

- ¾ cup chopped walnuts

- ¾ cup chopped macadamia nuts

DIRECTIONS

1. Preheat oven to 350°F. Lightly grease two 5x9-inch loaf pans.

2. In a bowl, mix the strawberries, pineapple, eggs, oil and sugar. In a separate bowl, sift together the flour, baking soda, salt, and cinnamon. Mix the flour mixture into the bowl with the fruit until evenly moist. Fold in walnuts and macadamia nuts. Divide the batter between the prepared loaf pans.

3. Bake loaves in the preheated oven until a toothpick inserted in the center of each loaf comes out clean, about 45-50 minutes. Cool on wire racks.

CAKES

APPLESAUCE SPICE CAKE

INGREDIENTS

Cake

- 2 ½ cups flour

- ½ tsp baking soda

- ½ tsp baking powder

- ¼ tsp salt

- ¾ tsp cinnamon

- ½ tsp ground cloves

- ½ tsp ground allspice

- ½ cup butter, softened 1 ¾ cups sugar

- ½ cup buttermilk

- 1 ½ cups applesauce

- 2 eggs

- ¾ cup chopped walnuts

Frosting

- ¼ cup butter

- cup chopped pecans

- cups confectioners' sugar 8 oz cream cheese, softened 1 ½ tsp vanilla extract

DIRECTIONS

1. Preheat oven to 350° (for dark pan, 325°). Mix all dry ingredients in a bowl. Cream the butter and sugar in a stand mixer. Add eggs, one at a time. Add buttermilk and applesauce and mix. Stir dry ingredients into butter mixture. Fold in walnuts. Pour into A 9x13" pan, and bake for 25 minutes.

2. When the cake comes out of the oven, melt the ¼ cup butter in a small pan. Add the pecans and stir until the butter is brown. Set aside to cool. Beat the cream cheese, confectioners' sugar and vanilla until smooth. Stir in the cooled pecans and frost the cooled cake.

BANANA-CHOCOLATE
CHIP SNACK CAKE

INGREDIENTS

- 2 cups (10 oz.) all-purpose flour

- ¾ teaspoon salt

- ½ teaspoon baking soda

- 8 tablespoons unsalted butter, softened

- 1½ cups (10½ oz.) sugar

- 2 large eggs

- 1 cup mashed ripe bananas (2 to 3 bananas)

- 1 teaspoon vanilla extract

- ½ cup whole milk

- 1 cup (6 oz.) semisweet chocolate chips

DIRECTIONS

1. Adjust oven rack to middle position and heat oven to 350°. Grease and flour 8-inch square baking pan. Wisk flour, salt, and baking soda together in a bowl.

2. Using a stand mixer fitted with paddle, beat butter and sugar on medium high speed until pale and fluffy, about 3 minutes. Add eggs, one at a time, and beat until combined. Add bananas and vanilla and beat until incorporated.

3. Reduce speed to low and add flour mixture in 3 additions, alternating with milk in 2 additions, scraping down bowl as needed. Using rubber spatula, stir in ½ cup chocolate chips. Transfer batter to prepared pan and smooth top with rubber spatula. Sprinkle remaining ½ cup chocolate chips evenly over the top. Bake until toothpick inserted comes out clean, 45-50 minutes, rotating pan halfway through baking.

4. Let cake cool completely in pan on wire rack. Serve. (Cooled cake can be wrapped in plastic wrap and stored at room temperature for up to 2 days)

CREAM CHEESE FROSTING

Use softened cream cheese to avoid lumps in the finished frosting.

- 4 tablespoons unsalted butter
- 1 cup (4 oz.) confectioner's sugar
- 4 oz. cream cheese, cut into 4 pieces and softened

- ¾ teaspoon vanilla extract

Using stand mixer fitted with paddle, beat butter and sugar on medium speed until light and fluffy, about 2 minutes. Add cream cheese, 1 piece at a time, beating after each addition until fully incorporated. Add vanilla and mix until no lumps remain.

BLUEBERRY MUFFIN STREUSEL CAKE

INGREDIENTS

For the cake:

- 1 cup all-purpose flour

- 1 ½ teaspoons baking powder

- ½ cup sugar

- ½ cup skim milk

- 1 egg

- 2 tablespoons canola oil

- 1 cup fresh blueberries

- Streusel Topping (recipe follows)

FOR THE STREUSEL TOPPING:

- ⅓ cup sugar

- ⅓ cup light brown sugar

- ½ cup all-purpose flour

- 2 teaspoons ground cinnamon

- 1 teaspoon vanilla extract

- 3 tablespoons butter, softened

- ½ cup chopped pecans

DIRECTIONS

For the cake:

1. Preheat oven 375°F. Coat 9x9x2-inch square pan with nonstick cooking pray

2. In bowl, mix together the oil, flour, baking powder, sugar, milk and egg.

3. Stir in blueberries, only until mixed.

4. Sprinkle ½ cup reserved Streusel Topping (see recipe) on bottom of pan. Carefully spread cake mixture on top. Cover with remaining reserved Streusel Pecan Topping.

5. Bake 20-25 minutes or until toothpick is inserted and comes out dry

For the streusel topping:

1. In small bowl, mix together sugar, brown sugar, flour and cinnamon.

2. Cut in vanilla and butter using pastry blender or fork.

3. Reserve ½ cup topping and add pecans to remaining topping.

CARROT CAKE WITH CREAM CHEESE FROSTING

INGREDIENTS

For Cake:

- ¼ cups canola oil

- 2 cups sugar

- 3 eggs

- 2 cups flour

- 2 teaspoons baking soda

- 1 teaspoon baking powder

- 2 teaspoons cinnamon

- 2 teaspoons vanilla extract

- 1 teaspoon salt

- 2 cups shredded carrots

- 1 cup chopped walnuts

- ½ cup raisins

- 8 ounces crushed pineapple

For Frosting:

- 8 oz. cream cheese, softened
- ½ cup butter, softened
- 1 lb confectioners sugar
- 1 teaspoon vanilla
- ¼ teaspoon salt

DIRECTIONS

1. Preheat oven to 350°.

2. Blend all cake ingredients with the mixer or by hand, and pour into a greased 9 x 13 pan.

3. Bake for 40 to 50 minutes or until a toothpick in the center comes out clean. Cool before frosting.

4. To make frosting: blend softened cream cheese and butter with the mixer. Add powdered sugar, vanilla and salt and beat well.

5. Frost cake as desired.

CHOCOLATE-CHERRY COLA CAKE

INGREDIENTS

- 1 jar (10 oz.) maraschino cherries, drained, ¼ cup liquid reserved

- 1 package devil's food cake mix

- 1 cup cherry cola carbonated beverage

- ½ cup vegetable oil

- 3 eggs

- 1 container (12 oz.) whipped vanilla frosting

DIRECTIONS

1. Preheat oven to 350°. Spray bottle only a 9 x 13 pan with baking spray. Chop cherries; set aside.

2. In a large bowl, beat cake mix, cola beverage, oil, eggs and ¼ cup reserved cherry liquid with an electric mixer on low speed for 30 seconds. Beat on medium speed two minutes.

3. Stir in chopped cherries. Pour into pan.

4. Bake 35 to 43 minutes or until tester comes out clean.

5. Cool completely on wire rack.

6. Frost cake and cut into 12 squares.

7. If desired top each square with two maraschino cherries with steps that have been drained well.

CINNAMON-APPLE CAKE

INGREDIENTS

- 1 ¾ cups sugar, divided
- ¾ cup (6 oz.) block-style fat-free cream cheese, softened
- ½ cup butter or stick margarine, softened
- I teaspoon vanilla extract
- 2 large eggs
- 1 ½ cups all-purpose flour
- 1 ½ teaspoons baking powder
- ¼ teaspoon salt
- 2 teaspoons ground cinnamon
- 3 cups chopped peeled Rome apple (about 2 large)
- Cooking spray

DIRECTIONS

1. Preheat oven to 350°.

2. Beat 1 ½ cups sugar, cream cheese, butter, and vanilla at medium speed of a mixer until well blended (about 4

minutes). Add eggs, 1 at a time, beating well after each addition; set aside.

3. Lightly spoon flour into dry measuring cups; level with a knife. Combine the flour, baking powder, and salt. Add flour mixture to creamed mixture, and beat at low speed until blended. Combine ¼ cup sugar and cinnamon. Combine 2 tablespoons of the cinnamon mixture and apple in a bowl; stir apple mixture into batter. Pour batter into an 8-inch spring form pan coated with cooking spray, and sprinkle with remaining cinnamon.

4. Bake at 350° for 1 hour and 15 minutes or until toothpick inserted in middle comes out clean. Cool completely on a wire rack, and cut using a serrated knife.

COCONUT CHAI COFFEE CAKE

INGREDIENTS

For Streusel:

- ½ cup butter, melted
- ½ cup flour
- ¾ cup brown sugar. packed
- 1 cup sweetened flaked coconut
- 1 teaspoon ground cardamom
- 1 teaspoon black pepper
- ½ teaspoon ground ginger
- ¼ teaspoon ground cloves
- ½ tsp salt

For Cake:

- 2 cups flour
- 1 ½ teaspoons baking powder
- ½ teaspoon baking soda
- ½ teaspoon salt
- 1 ½ cups brown sugar, packed

- ½ cup butter, room temperature

- 1 cup sour cream

- 2 eggs

- 1 teaspoon vanilla

DIRECTIONS

1. Preheat oven to 350°. Coat a 9-inch spring form pan with butter and flour. Set aside.

2. Combine all streusel ingredients in a small bowl and mix until clumpy and well incorporated. Place in the fridge until you're ready to use. To make the cake, whisk together the flour, baking powder, baking soda and salt in a large bowl. Cream together the brown sugar and the butter in another bowl using an electric mixer. Add the sour cream and mix well, then add the eggs and vanilla and blend until combined.

3. Add the dry ingredients to the wet ingredients and mix until just combined, then transfer the batter into your prepared pan and spread evenly. Remove the streusel from the fridge and scatter it on top of the cake, pressing gently so it adheres to the batter. Bake the coffee cake for 50 to 55 minutes. Transfer to a rack and let cool for 20 minutes before slicing and serving.

CRANBERRY-ORANGE CRUMB CAKE

For the crumbs

- 8 tablespoons (1 stick) unsalted butter

- ⅓ cup dark brown sugar

- ¼ cup sugar

- 1 ½ teaspoons ground cinnamon

- ¼ teaspoon salt

- 1 ¼ cup all-purpose flour

For the cake

- 1 cup all-purpose flour

- ½ teaspoon baking soda

- ½ teaspoon baking powder

- ¼ teaspoon salt

- 5 tablespoons unsalted butter, at room temperature

- ½ cup sugar

- 1 teaspoon pure vanilla extract

- 1 large egg, at room temperature

- ½ cup sour cream

- I tablespoon orange zest

- 1 cup fresh or frozen cranberries

DIRECTIONS

1. Preheat the oven to 350° F. Line a square 8 x 8-inch pan with parchment paper, leaving extra overhang.

2. For the crumbs: In a medium saucepan over low heat, combine the butter, sugars, cinnamon and salt. When the butter is melted, turn off the heat and stir in the flour. Set aside to cool. In a medium bowl, whisk together the flour, baking soda, baking powder and salt.

3. In a large bowl, cream the butter and sugar together with an electric mixer until light and fluffy. Add the vanilla, egg, sour cream and zest, and mix until incorporated. Add the dry ingredients and mix until fully combined. Fold in the cranberries.

4. Transfer the batter to the prepared pan and use a spatula to spread (it will be thick). With your hands, form small to medium-sized balls with the crumb mixture and scatter on top of the batter. Bake in the oven until a toothpick

inserted into the center comes out clean, 45-55 minutes. The crumbs should be golden brown and feel firm. If they begin to look too brown cover with a piece of foil until the cake is done.

EGGNOG COFFEE CAKE

INGREDIENTS

Cake

- 1 cup (2 sticks) unsalted butter (at room temperature)
- ½ cup Crisco
- 3 cup Sugar
- 5 large eggs- at room temperature
- 2 tbsp Spiced rum (optional or substitute with Vanilla extract)
- 3 cup All-purpose flour
- 2 tsp Nutmeg
- ½ tsp Baking powder
- Pinch of salt
- 1¼ cup eggnog

Streusel

- ¾ cup Flour
- ¼ cup brown sugar
- ½ cup (1 stick) Unsalted butter

DIRECTIONS

1. Preheat oven to 325°.

2. Allow eggs and butter to come to room temperature. Cream together the butter, and Crisco until smooth. Beat in sugar and cream it until well blended. Don't rush this step; allow to beat for at least 5 minutes.

3. Slowly add eggs 1 at a time and make sure each one is well mixed.

4. Once all eggs have been blended into the batter, add rum and mix to combine. Scrape down the sides of the bowls.

5. In a separate bowl, sift flour first and then measure out 3 cups.

6. Add half of the dry ingredients and then half of the eggnog and mix until combined. Add the second half of your dry ingredients, followed by the remaining eggnog. Continue to beat until all ingredients are well combined.

7. Pour batter into a 9" x 13" pan.

8. Prepare the streusel by combining the flour and brown sugar together. Cut the butter into smaller pieces and then crush into the flour mixture with a pastry cutter or a couple of forks. Mash together until the butter is

crumbled into the flour. You will add the streusel after 30 minutes of baking.

9. Bake at 325° for 65-72 minutes. Set the timer for 30 minutes. Open the oven and sprinkle the streusel on top.

10. After about 45 minutes of baking, the cake will start to brown on top. You can cover with tin foil for 10-15 minutes. Then remove for the foil for the last few minutes.

11. Check to see if your cake is done by inserting a toothpick into the middle. If it comes out clean, your cake is done. Baking times may vary by oven. Allow to cool before cutting.

FRENCH APPLE CAKE

INGREDIENTS

- 1 cup all-purpose flour, spooned into measuring cup and leveled-off

- 1 teaspoon baking powder

- ¼ teaspoon salt

- 1 stick (½ cup) unsalted butter, at room temperature

- ⅔ cup granulated sugar, plus more for sprinkling over cake

- 2 large eggs

- 1 teaspoon vanilla extract

- 3 tablespoons dark rum

- 2 sweet baking apples, peeled, cored and cut into ½-inch cubes

- Confectioner's sugar (optional), for decorating cake

DIRECTIONS

1. Preheat the oven to 350°F. Spray a 9-inch spring form or regular cake pan with nonstick cooking spray.

2. In a small bowl, whisk together the flour, baking powder and salt.

3. Using a handheld mixer with beaters or a stand mixer with the paddle attachment, cream the butter and granulated sugar until light and fluffy, about 3 minutes.

4. Add the eggs, one at a time, beating well and scraping down the sides of the bowl after each addition. Beat in the vanilla and rum. Don't worry if the batter looks grainy.

5. Add the flour mixture and mix on low speed until just combined. Using a rubber spatula, fold in the chopped apples.

6. Pour the batter into the prepared pan and sprinkle evenly with 1 tablespoon of granulated sugar.

7. Bake for about 40 minutes, or until the cake is lightly golden and a toothpick inserted into the center comes out clean.

8. Allow the cake to cool until just warm. Run a blunt knife around the edges of the cake and remove the sides of the spring form pan if using.

Using a fine sieve, dust with Confectioners' sugar (if using). Cake can be served warm or room temperature, with or without lightly sweetened whipped cream or vanilla ice cream.

FROSTED ORANGE CAKE

INGREDIENTS

- 1 large orange

- 1 cup orange juice

- 1 pkg (18.25 oz) plain yellow cake mix

- 1 pkg (3.4 oz) vanilla instant pudding mix

- ½ c vegetable oil

- 1 tsp vanilla extract

- 3 large eggs

- Orange Cream Cheese Frosting (see below)

DIRECTIONS

1. Preheat the oven to 325°. Spray a 9 x 13" pan with baking spray.

2. Grate the orange zest. Squeeze the juice into a measuring cup. Add enough juice from the carton to measure 1 ⅓ cups.

3. Place the cake mix, pudding mix, oil, vanilla, eggs and orange juice in a large mixing bowl. Beat on low speed until the ingredients are moistened. Increase the speed to medium and mix 1 ½ minutes longer.

4. Put cake batter into prepared pan, smoothing the top. Bake for 25 minutes or until the top springs back when lightly touched. Let cool completely.

Orange Cream Cheese Frosting

- 1 stick of butter, at room temperature

- 4 oz. cream cheese, at room temperature

- 1 tsp grated orange zest from a small orange 2-3 tsp fresh orange juice

- 3 cups confectioners' sugar (may need more)

1. Beat the butter and cream cheese in a medium-sized bowl until combined.

2. Add the orange zest, 2 tsp of the orange juice and the confectioners' sugar.

3. Beat on low speed until incorporated, then on medium speed until fluffy.

FRUIT SMOOTHIE NO-BAKE CHEESECAKE

INGREDIENTS

- 1 ½ cups graham cracker crumbs

- ¼ cup (½ stick) butter, melted

- 2 tbsp sugar

- 4 pkg. (8oz each) cream cheese, softened

- ½ cup sugar

- 12 oz frozen mixed berries, thawed and drained

- 8 oz whipped topping, thawed, divided

DIRECTIONS

1. Line a 9x13 baking pan with foil, with ends of foil extending over sides of pan. Mix graham cracker crumbs, butter and 2 tbsp sugar; press firmly into bottom of prepared pan. Refrigerate while preparing filling.

2. Beat cream cheese and ½ cup sugar in large bowl with electric mixer at medium speed until well blended. Smash drained berries with a fork and stir into cheese mixture. Gently stir in 2 cups of the whipped topping. Spoon over crust and cover.

3. Refrigerate 4 hours or until firm. Use foil handles to remove cheesecake from pan before cutting to serve. Top with the remaining whipped topping. Store leftover cheesecake in refrigerator.

LUSCIOUS LEMON CAKE

INGREDIENTS

Cake

- 1 (18 ¼ ounce) packages lemon cake mix (Duncan Hines Lemon Supreme)

- 4 eggs

- 1 (15 ounce) cans lemon pie filling

Frosting

- 1 (8 oz) packages cream cheese, softened ½ cup butter, softened (1 stick)

- 2 cups confectioners' sugar

- 1 ½ teaspoons vanilla (I use 2 tsp, as I really like vanilla)

DIRECTIONS

1. For the cake, beat the cake mix and eggs until blended using a mixer on low.

2. Fold in lemon pie filling (do not beat in).

64

3. Spread in a greased 13 x 9-inch pan and bake at 350° for 20-25 minutes. (You might also want to put parchment paper on the bottom, greased on both sides, for easy removal.).

4. For the frosting, mix the butter and cream cheese until smooth using the mixer on low.

5. Add the sugar and vanilla, again blending until smooth.

6. You can frost the cake once it has cooled, but if you want to frost it later (or make the frosting ahead of time), you can store it in the refrigerator in a bowl with plastic wrap applied directly on top of the frosting. Make sure it is covered completely, and it will last in the fridge for a couple days.

OATMEAL WALNUT CARAMEL COFFEE CAKE

INGREDIENTS

- 1½ cups all-purpose flour

- 1 teaspoon baking powder

- 1 teaspoon salt

- ½ teaspoon ground cinnamon

- ¾ cup quick-cooking oats SC

- 6 tablespoons salted-butter, softened

- 1 cup packed brown sugar

- 3 large eggs

- 1 teaspoon vanilla extract

- ½ cup chopped and toasted walnuts or pecans

- ½ cup salted caramel sauce, slightly warmed just enough to loosen for easy drizzling

DIRECTIONS

1. Preheat the oven to 350° Fahrenheit. Prepare an 8-inch square baking pan with cooking spray or butter. Lightly whisk together the flour, baking powder, and salt, then, whisk in oats; set aside. Beat together the butter and sugar until well blended. Add eggs and vanilla, mixing well. Scrape down the sides when needed.

2. Mix in the dry ingredient mixture until just combined, and stir in walnuts to distribute. Evenly spread the batter in your prepared baking pan. Drizzle the caramel sauce over the top of the batter. Using a knife, swirl caramel throughout the batter. Spread the batter evenly again.

3. Bake at 350° Fahrenheit for 40 minutes, or until a wooden pick or cake tester comes out clean. Cool the pan on a wire rack. Note: Adjust the cook time based on your pan size.

PINA COLADA CAKE

INGREDIENTS

- 1 (18 ¼ or 18 ½ ounce) package yellow cake mix
- 1 (4 serving size) package instant vanilla flavor pudding mix
- 1 (15ounce) can Coco Lopez® Cream of Coconut
- ½ cup plus 2 tablespoons rum
- ⅓ cup vegetable oil
- 4 eggs
- 1 (8 ounce) can crushed pineapple, well drained
- Whipped Topping (optional)

DIRECTIONS

1. Preheat oven to 350° F.

2. In a large mixer bowl, combine cake mix, pudding mix, ½ cup cream of coconut, ½ cup of rum, oil and eggs. Beat on a medium speed for 2 minutes. Stir in the pineapple.

3. Pour into well-greased and floured 10-inch fluted tube or tube pan. Bake 50 to 55 minutes. Cool 10 minutes. Remove from pan.

4. With a table knife or skewer, poke holes about 1 inch apart in cake almost to bottom. Combine remaining cream of coconut and remaining 2 tablespoons of rum; slowly spoon over cake.

5. Chill thoroughly. Garnishing as desired. Store in refrigerator.

TIRAMISU CHEESECAKE
DESSERT RECIPE

INGREDIENTS

- 1 package (12 oz.) vanilla wafers
- 5 teaspoons instant coffee granules, divided
- 3 tablespoons hot water, divided
- 4 packages (8 oz. each) cream cheese, softened
- 1 cup sugar
- 1 cup (8 oz.) sour cream
- 4 large eggs, lightly beaten
- 1 cup whipped topping
- 1 tablespoon baking cocoa

DIRECTIONS

1. Preheat oven to 325°. Layer half of the wafers in a greased 13X9-in. baking dish. In a small bowl, dissolve 2 teaspoons coffee granules in 2 tablespoons hot water; brush 1 tablespoon mixture over wafers.

2. In a large bowl, beat cream cheese and sugar until smooth. Beat in sour cream. Add eggs; beat on low speed just until blended. Remove half of the filling to another bowl. Dissolve remaining coffee granules in remaining hot water; stir into one portion of filling. Spread over wafers.

3. Layer remaining wafers over top; brush with remaining dissolved granules. Spread with remaining filling.

4. Bake 40-45 minutes or until center is almost set. Cool on a wire rack 10 minutes. Loosen sides from dish with a knife. Cool 1 hour or longer. Refrigerate overnight, covering when completely cooled.

5. To serve, spread with whipped topping. Dust with cocoa. Yield: 12 servings.

TROPICAL COCONUT CRUMB CAKE

INGREDIENTS

For the crumbs:

- 1 cup packed light brown sugar

- ½ cup all-purpose flour

- ¼ teaspoon salt

- ½ cup shredded sweetened coconut

- 4 tablespoons unsalted butter, melted

For the cake:

- 1 ½ cups all-purpose flour

- 1 ½ teaspoons baking powder

- ¼ teaspoon salt

- 8 tablespoons (1 stick) unsalted butter, at room temperature

- ¾ cup sugar

- 2 large eggs, at room temperature

- 1 teaspoon pure vanilla extract

- ½ teaspoon coconut extract

- ¾ cup light coconut milk - shake well before using

DIRECTIONS

1. Preheat the oven to 350° F. Line an 8 x 8-inch square pan with parchment paper, leaving overhang and set aside.

2. For the crumbs: In a medium bowl, combine the sugar, flour, salt and coconut flakes. Mix until well combined. Pour the melted butter over the mixture. Stir together until combined. Set aside until ready to use.

3. In another medium bowl, whisk together the flour, baking powder and salt.

4. In a large bowl, cream the butter and sugar together with an electric mixer until light and fluffy. Add the eggs, vanilla and coconut extract, and mix until incorporated. Alternate between adding the dry ingredients and coconut milk, finishing with the flour mixture.

5. Transfer the batter to the prepared pan and use a spatula to spread. With your hands, form small to medium-sized balls with the crumb mixture and scatter on top of the batter. Bake in the oven until a toothpick inserted into the center comes out clean, about 40 minutes. If the crumbs

begin to brown too quickly, cover with a piece of foil until the cake is done

6. Cool in the pan until the cake is just warm. Grasp the parchment paper with both hands and lift the cake out of the pan. Cut into 9 squares.

BEST-EVER BOURBON BROWNIES

INGREDIENTS

- ½ cup butter
- ½ cup granulated sugar
- 2 tablespoons water
- 1 cup semisweet chocolate pieces
- 2 eggs
- 1 teaspoon vanilla
- ¾ cup all-purpose flour
- ¼ teaspoon baking soda
- ¼ teaspoon salt
- ½ cup chopped pecans
- 2 to 3 tablespoons bourbon
- 3 tablespoons butter, softened
- 1½ cups sifted powdered sugar
- 2 -3 teaspoons milk
- ¼ teaspoon vanilla

- 1-ounce semisweet chocolate, melted

DIRECTIONS

1. Grease an 8 x 8 x 2-inch baking pan; set aside. In a medium saucepan, combine ⅓ cup butter, the granulated sugar, and water. Cook and stir over medium heat just until boiling. Remove from heat. Add the 1 cup chocolate pieces; stir until chocolate is melted. Stir in eggs and vanilla, beating lightly with a spoon just until combined. Stir in flour, baking soda, and salt. Stir in pecans. Spread batter into prepared pan.

2. Bake in a 350°F oven about 20 minutes or until edges are set and begin to pull away from sides of pan.

3. Using a fork, prick the warm brownies several times. Drizzle bourbon evenly over brownies; cool in pan on a wire rack.

4. For frosting, in a small mixing bowl beat the 3 tablespoons butter with an electric mixer on medium to high speed for 30 seconds. Gradually add powdered sugar, beating well. Slowly beat in 2 teaspoons of the milk and vanilla. If necessary, beat in remaining milk to reach spreading consistency. Spread over brownies; drizzle melted chocolate over frosting.

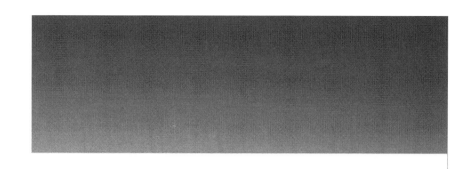

COOKIES

BUCKEYE COOKIE BARS

INGREDIENTS

- 1 package chocolate cake mix
- ¼ cup vegetable oil
- 1 egg
- 1 cup chopped peanuts
- 1 (14 ounce) can sweetened condensed milk
- ½ cup peanut butter

DIRECTIONS

1. Preheat oven to 350°. Grease a 9 x 13 pan.

2. In a large mixing bowl, combine cake mix, oil and egg, beat on medium speed until crumbly. Stir in peanuts.

3. Reserving 1 ½ cups crumb mixture, press remainder on bottom prepared.

4. In medium bowl, beat sweetened condensed milk with peanut butter until smooth. Spread over crust. Sprinkle with reserved crumb mixture.

5. Bake 25 to 30 minutes or until set. Cool. Cut into 24 to 36 bars. Store loosely covered at room temperature.

BUTTER-PECAN BLONDIES

INGREDIENTS

- 1½ cups whole pecans

- 2 sticks unsalted butter, melted, plus more for brushing

- 2 cups unbleached all-purpose flour, plus more for dusting

- 1 ¼ teaspoons kosher salt

- 2 cups light-brown sugar, plus 2 tablespoons for sprinkling

- 2 large eggs, room temperature

- 1 tablespoon pure vanilla extract

- 1 tablespoon dark rum (optional)

DIRECTIONS

1. Preheat oven to 350 degrees F. Spread pecans on a rimmed baking sheet; toast until fragrant, 6 to 7 minutes. Let cool, then chop.

2. Brush a 9x13-inch baking dish with butter, then dust with flour, tapping out excess. In a medium bowl, whisk

together flour and salt. In a large bowl, whisk together butter and 2 cups brown sugar until combined. Add eggs; whisk until combined. Add vanilla and rum. Fold in flour mixture with a spatula until just combined (do not over-mix). Fold in half of nuts.

3. Transfer batter to prepared dish; smooth top with an offset spatula. Sprinkle top with remaining nuts and 2 tablespoons brown sugar. Bake until golden around edges and a tester inserted in center comes out with very few crumbs, 20-25 minutes.

4. Transfer to a wire rack and let cool completely before cutting into squares. Blondies can be stored in an airtight container at room temperature up to 3 days.

CARAMEL AND CHOCOLATE PECAN BARS

INGREDIENTS

Crust

- 2 cups flour

- 1 cup packed brown sugar

- ½ cup butter

- 1 cup pecan halves

Topping

- ⅔ cup butter

- ½ cup packed brown sugar

- 1 cup semisweet chocolate chips

DIRECTIONS

1. Preheat oven to 350°. Combine all crust ingredients except pecans in a bowl.

2. Beat at medium speed until mixture resembles fine crumbs. Press on the bottom of ungreased 9 x 13 pan. Place pecans evenly over unbaked crust.

3. Combine ⅔ cup butter and ½ cup brown sugar in 1-quart saucepan. Cook over medium heat, stirring constantly until entire surface of mixture begins to boil.

4. Boil, stirring constantly, one minute. Pour mixture evenly over pecans and crust.

5. Bake 18 to 22 minutes or until entire caramel layer is bubbly.

6. Remove from oven. Immediately sprinkle with chips; allowed to melt slightly. Swirl melted chips over bars leaving some hold for marbled cool completely. Cut into 36 bars.

CHOCOLATE-GLAZED TOFFEE BARS

INGREDIENTS

Dough

- ⅔ cup flour

- 1 ½ tbsp. sugar

- ⅛ tsp. kosher salt

- 4 tbsp. unsalted butter, cubed and chilled

- 2 tsp. milk

Toffee and Chocolate Layers

- ½ cup packed light brown sugar

- 6 tbsp. unsalted butter

- 2 tbsp. honey

- 1 tbsp. milk

- ⅛ tsp. kosher salt

- 1 ¾ cups finely chopped pecans, lightly toasted

- 1 tsp. vanilla extract

- ¼ cup semisweet chocolate chips

DIRECTIONS

1. Heat oven to 350 degrees.

2. Make the crust: Whisk flour, sugar and salt in a bowl. Add butter and using a dough blender, two forks, or your fingers, cut butter into flour mixture, forming pea-size crumbles; stir in milk until dough forms. Add more milk, if necessary, until dough holds together but is not wet. Press dough into a parchment paper lined 8" square baking dish; chill 15 minutes.

3. Bake crust until golden, 20 minutes; let cool.

4. Make the toffee layer: Bring sugar, butter, honey, milk, and salt to a boil in a 2-qt. saucepan over medium heat. Cook until sugar is dissolved and butter is melted, about 3 minutes.

5. Remove from heat; stir in 1 ½ cups pecans and the vanilla.

6. Spread toffee mixture evenly over the crust; bake until toffee is golden brown and bubbly, 17-20 minutes. Transfer the pan to a wire rack; let cool 5 minutes, then sprinkle evenly with chocolate chips.

7. Let stand 5 minutes, then, using a spatula, smooth chocolate into an even layer; sprinkle immediately with remaining pecans. Let cool completely, and then refrigerate until firm; cut into squares.

CHOCOLATE MACAROON SQUARES

INGREDIENTS

- 1 package chocolate cake mix
- ⅓ cup butter, softened
- 1 large egg, lightly beaten
- 14 ounce can sweetened condensed milk
- 1 large egg
- 1 teaspoon vanilla extract
- ⅓ cups flaked sweet coconut, divided
- 1 cup chopped pecans
- 1 cup (6 ounce) semisweet chocolate chips

DIRECTIONS

1. Preheat oven to 350°.

2. Combine cake mix, butter and egg in large bowl; mix with a fork until crumbly.

3. Press on the bottom of ungreased 9 x 13 pan.

4. Combine sweetened condensed milk, egg and vanilla extract in a medium bowl; beat until well blended. Stir in 1 cup coconut, nuts and chocolate chips.

5. Spread mixture evenly over base; sprinkle with remaining coconut.

6. Bake 20 to 30 minutes or until center is almost set. Cool in pan on wire rack. Cut into 24 squares.

COFFEE & COOKIE BROWNIES

INGREDIENTS

- 1 pkg refrigerated sugar cookie dough

- 2 eggs, lightly beaten

- 1 pkg. milk chocolate brownie mix

- ½ cup vegetable oil

- ⅓ cup coffee liqueur, or cooked strong coffee

- 1 cup semisweet or bittersweet chocolate pieces

DIRECTIONS

1. Preheat oven to 350 degrees. Press cookie dough down into the bottom of a 9x13 pan, set aside.

2. In a large bowl combine eggs, brownie mix, oil coffee liqueur until just combined. Spread the batter over sugar cookies dough. Sprinkle with chocolate pieces.

3. Bake 40 minutes or until edges are set. Cool in pan on wire rack. Cut into 24 brownies.

CRANBERRY COCONUT OAT BARS

INGREDIENTS

- ½ cup butter, melted
- ⅓ cup granulated sugar
- 1 cup all-purpose flour
- ½ cup quick-cooking rolled oats
- 2 eggs
- 1 cup packed brown sugar
- ⅓ cup all-purpose flour
- 1 tsp baking powder
- ¾ tsp cinnamon
- 1 ⅓ cups dried cranberries
- 1 cup unsweetened flaked coconut

DIRECTIONS

1. Preheat oven to 350°F.

2. Crust: In a bowl, com bine melted butter, sugar, flour and oats, mixing well. Press evenly into prepared pan. Bake in

preheated oven until lightly browned, about 15 minutes. Let cool in pan on rack.

3. Topping: In a large bowl, whisk eggs and brown sugar until blended. Whisk in flour, baking powder and cinnamon until blended. Stir in dried cranberries and coconut. Spread evenly over cooled base.

4. Return to oven and bake until set and golden, 20 to 25 minutes. Let cool completely in pan on rack. Cut into bars.

GERMAN CHOCOLATE
PECAN PIE BARS

INGREDIENTS

- 3 cups pecan halves

- 1 ¾ cups all-purpose flour

- ¾ cup confectioners' sugar

- ¾ cup cold butter, cubed

- ¼ cup unsweetened cocoa powder

- 1 ½ cups semisweet chocolate chips

- 3 large eggs

- ¾ cup firmly packed light brown sugar

- ¾ cup light corn syrup

- ¼ cup unsalted butter, melted

- 1 cup sweetened flaked coconut

DIRECTIONS

1. Preheat oven to 350°F.

2. Arrange pecans in a single layer of a shallow baking pan. Bake 8-10 minutes or until lightly toasted. Stir halfway through baking.

3. Line the bottom and sides of a 9"x 13 "x 2" baking pan with aluminum foil, leaving an overhang on two short sides. Grease foil.

4. Whisk together the flour, confectioners' sugar, and cocoa. Add the cold butter, and combine with a pastry blender until the mixture resembles coarse meal. Press the mixture into the bottom and about ¾-inch up sides of prepared pan.

5. Bake the crust for 15 minutes. Remove from oven and immediately sprinkle chocolate chips evenly over crust. Allow to cool on a wire rack at least 30 minutes.

6. Place the eggs in a large mixing bowl, and beat lightly. Add the brown sugar, corn syrup, and melted butter. Whisk together until smooth. Stir in the coconut and pecans. Pour evenly over the partially baked crust.

7. Bake 28-34 minutes, or until the edges are golden and the filling has set. Cool completely on a wire rack. Then, refrigerate for an hour.

8. Using foil overhang, lift the bars from the pan and place on a cutting board. Use a sharp knife to cut into bars.

DEEP DARK FUDGY BROWNIES

INGREDIENTS

- 2/ 3 cup Dutch-process cocoa
- 1 ½ cups granulated sugar
- ½ cup confectioners' sugar
- ¼ teaspoon salt
- 1 cup Unbleached All-Purpose Flour
- 1 ½ teaspoons espresso powder
- 1 cup (4 ounces) chopped toasted pecans or walnuts (optional)
- 1 cup (6 ounces) semisweet chocolate chips
- ½ cup vegetable oil
- 2 tablespoons water or cold brewed coffee
- 3 large eggs

DIRECTIONS

1. Preheat the oven to 350°F. Lightly grease an 8" or 9"square pan.

2. In a large bowl, whisk together the cocoa, sugars, salt, flour, espresso powder, nuts (if using), and chocolate. Stir in the oil, water (or coffee), and eggs, mixing until combined.

3. Spread the batter in the prepared pan, smoothing the top.

4. Bake for 33 to 35 minutes for the 9" pan, or 40 to 45 minutes for the 8" pan. Test for doneness by inserting a paring knife in the center. If it's coated with batter, give the brownies another 5 minutes and test again. The tip of the knife should come out with moist crumbs clinging to it.

5. When done, remove the brownies from the oven and cool on a rack for at least 1 hour before cutting.

KEY LIME BARS

INGREDIENTS

<u>Crust</u>

- 5 ounces animal crackers

- 3 tablespoons packed brown sugar

- pinch table salt

- 4 tablespoons unsalted butter, melted, cool slightly

<u>Filling</u>

- 2 ounces cream cheese, softened

- 1 tablespoon grated lime zest, minced

- page table salt

- 14 ounces sweetened condensed milk

- one large egg yolk

- ½ cup lime juice or key lime juice

DIRECTIONS

1. Preheat oven to 325°. Line an 8 in. square pan with heavy duty foil. Spray foil with baking spray.

2. In a food processor, pulse animal crackers to even, fine crumb. Add brown sugar and salt; process to combine. Drizzle butter over crumbs and pulse until evenly moistened.

3. Press crimes evenly and firmly into the bottom of prepared pan. Bake 18 to 20 minutes or until deep golden brown. Cool on wire rack while making. Do not turn off oven.

4. While crust cools, in a medium bowl, stir cream cheese, zest, and salt with rubber spatula until cleanly and thoroughly combined.

5. Add sweetened and condensed milk and whisk vigorously until no lumps of cream cheese remain; whisk in egg yolk.

6. Add line or key lime juice and whisk until blended. Pour filling onto crust, spreading to corners.

7. Bake until set and edges begin to pull away slightly from sides, 15 to 20 minutes.

8. Cool on wire rack to room temperature. Cover with foil and refrigerate until thoroughly chilled. Remove from pan by lifting foil and cut into (16) 2-inch bars.

MIXED BERRY CRUMBLE BARS

INGREDIENTS

Crust and Topping

- 1 cup granulated sugar

- 1 teaspoon baking powder

- 3 cups all-purpose flour

- ¼ teaspoon salt

- Finely grated zest of 1 small lemon (optional)

- 1 cup cold unsalted butter cut into cubes

- 1 large egg

- ½ teaspoon pure vanilla extract

Berry Filling

- 4 ½ cups chopped fresh berries (raspberries, blackberries, blueberries, etc.)

- ½ cup granulated sugar

- 4 teaspoons cornstarch

- Juice of 1 small lemon

DIRECTIONS

Preheat oven to 350°F. Line a 9x13 pan with foil or parchment, and butter or spray with non-stick spray.

For the crust and topping:

1. Using a hand mixer or stand mixer fitted with the paddle attachment, combine granulated sugar, baking powder, flour, and salt. Add lemon zest, butter, egg, and vanilla. Beat on low speed until the butter is evenly distributed in small pieces and the mixture is crumbly.

2. Dump a little more than half of the mixture into the bottom of the prepared pan. Use your hand or the bottom of a measuring cup to evenly press the dough into the pan.

Filling

1. Gently stir together all ingredients until well incorporated.

2. Spread the filling over the crust, then crumble the remaining dough over the top of the berries.

3. Bake for approximately 40 minutes, until the top is light golden brown. Transfer pan to rack to cool, before cutting into squares. You can refrigerate these after cooling to room temperature.

NANAIMO BARS

INGREDIENTS

- ½ cup butter, softened
- ¼ cup white sugar
- 5 tablespoons unsweetened cocoa powder
- 1 egg, beaten
- 1 ¾ cups graham cracker crumbs
- 1 cup flaked coconut
- ½ cup finely chopped almonds (optional)
- ½ cup butter, softened
- 3 tablespoons heavy cream
- 2 tablespoons custard powder
- 2 cups confectioners' sugar
- 4 (1 ounce) squares semisweet baking chocolate
- 2 teaspoons butter

DIRECTIONS

1. In the top of a double boiler, combine ½ cup butter, white sugar and cocoa powder. Stir occasionally until melted and smooth. Beat in the egg, stirring until thick, 2 to 3 minutes. Remove from heat and mix in the graham cracker crumbs, coconut and almonds (if you like). Press into the bottom of an ungreased 8x8 inch pan.

2. For the middle layer, cream together ½ cup butter, heavy cream and custard powder until light and fluffy. Mix in the confectioners' sugar until smooth. Spread over the bottom layer in the pan. Chill to set.

3. While the second layer is chilling, melt the semisweet chocolate and 2 teaspoons butter together in the microwave over low heat. Spread over the chilled bars. Let the chocolate set before cutting into squares.

NO-BAKE CHOCOLATE PEANUT BUTTER BARS

INGREDIENTS

- ½ cup salted butter, melted*

- 1 cup graham cracker crumbs (about 8 full sheet graham crackers)

- 2 cups confectioners' sugar

- 1 cup + 2 Tbsp creamy peanut butter, divided

- 1 cup semi-sweet chocolate chips

DIRECTIONS

1. Line an 8x8 or 9x9 inch square baking pan with aluminum foil or parchment paper. Set aside.

2. Mix the melted butter, graham cracker crumbs, and confectioners' sugar together in a medium bowl. Stir in 1 cup of peanut butter, then spread evenly into prepared baking pan.

3. Melt remaining 2 Tablespoons of peanut butter with the chocolate chips in the microwave or on the stove. Stir until smooth. Spread over peanut butter layer.

4. Chill in the refrigerator until completely firm, at least 2 hours. Allow to sit at room temperature for 10 minutes before cutting. Serve chilled.

5. Setting them out for a few hours at room temperature for serving is OK.

PECAN PIE BARS

INGREDIENTS

Crust

- 1 ½ sticks unsalted butter

- 2 cups flour

- ½ cup packed light brown sugar

- ½ teaspoon salt

Filling

- 8 ounces pecans (about 2 cups)

- 1 stick unsalted butter

- 1 cup packed light brown sugar

- ⅓ cup honey

- 2 tablespoons heavy cream

DIRECTIONS

1. Preheat oven to 350°. Cut butter into half inch pieces.

2. In a food processor process all crust ingredients until mixture begins to form small clumps. Sprinkle mixture into a 9 x 13 pan and press evenly onto bottom.

3. Bake about 20 minutes or until golden brown. While crust is baking prepare topping.

4. Coarsely chop pecans. In a heavy saucepan, melt butter and stir in brown sugar, honey, and cream.

5. Simmer mixture, stirring occasionally, about 1 minute. Stir in pecans.

6. Poor pecan mixture over hot crust and spread evenly.

7. Bake until bubbling, about 20 minutes. Cool completely in pan and cut into 24 bars.

RASPBERRY STREUSEL BARS

INGREDIENTS

- 2 ½ cups flour

- ⅔ cup sugar

- ½ teaspoon salt

- 18 tablespoons unsalted butter, cut into half-inch pieces and softened, divided

- ¼ cup packed brown sugar

- ½ cup old-fashioned rolled oats

- ½ cup pecans, chopped fine

- ¾ cup raspberry preserves

- 1 tablespoon lemon juice

DIRECTIONS

1. Preheat oven to 375°. Line a 9 x 13 pan with foil. Allow access to overhang pan edges. Spray foil lined pan with baking spray.

2. Mix flour, granulated sugar, and salt at low speed until combined, about five seconds.

3. With machine on low, at 16 tablespoons butter one piece at a time; then continue mixing on low until mixture resembles dancing, 1-1 ½ minutes.

4. Remove 1 ¼ cup of mixture to a medium bowl and reserve. Press remaining mixture evenly in bottom of prepared pan.

5. Bake until edges begin to brown, 14 to 18 minutes.

6. While crust is baking, add brown sugar, oats and nuts to reserve flour mixture; toss to combine.

7. Working remaining 2 tablespoons butter by rubbing mixture between fingers until butter is fully incorporated. Pinch mixture with fingers to create hazelnut size clumps, set streusel aside.

8. Combine preserves, raspberries, and lemon juice in a small bowl; mash with a fork until combined but some berry pieces remain. Spread filling evenly over hot crust; sprinkle streusel topping evenly over filling.

9. Return panda oven and bake until topping is golden brown filling is bubbly, 20-25 minutes.

10. Cool to room temperature on wire rack, remove from baking pan by lifting foil extensions. Cut into 24 squares.

THICK AND CHEWEY
CHOCOLATE CHIP BARS

INGREDIENTS

- 2 ⅛ cups flour

- ½ teaspoon salt

- ½ teaspoon baking soda

- 1 ½ sticks unsalted butter, melted and cooled slightly

- 1 cup light brown sugar, packed

- ½ cup granulated sugar

- 1 large egg

- 1 large egg yolk

- 2 teaspoons vanilla extract

- 2 cups chocolate chips or chunks (semi-or bittersweet)

DIRECTIONS

1. Preheat oven to 325°. Line a 9 x 13 pan with foil leaving edges over. Spray foil with baking spray.

2. Mix flour, salt, and baking soda together in medium bowl, set aside.

3. Whisk melted butter and sugar in large bowl until combined. Add egg, egg yolk, and vanilla and mix well.

4. Using spatula, full dry ingredients in the egg mixture until just combined; do not overmix.

5. Fold in chips and turned batter onto prepared pan, smoothing topless spatula.

6. Bake 27-30 minutes, or until top is light golden brown, slightly firm to the touch, and edges start pulling away from sides of pan. Cool on wire rack to room temperature. Lift foil overhang to remove bars and cut into 24 squares

TURTLE BROWNIES

INGREDIENTS

- 4 squares unsweetened baking chocolate

- 1 ½ sticks butter

- 2 cups sugar

- 4 eggs

- 1 cup flour

- 1 package (14 ounces) caramels, unwrapped

- ⅓ cup heavy cream

- 2 cups pecans or walnuts, divided

- 1 package (12 ounces) semisweet chocolate chips

DIRECTIONS

1. Preheat oven to 350°. Spray foil line 9 x 13 pan with baking spray.

2. Microwave chocolate and butter on high 2 minutes or until butter is melted. Stir until chocolate is completely melted.

3. Stir sugar into chocolate until blended. Mix in eggs and stir in flour.

4. Spread half batter and prepared pan. Bake 25 minutes, or until batter is firm to the touch.

5. Microwave caramels and cream on high 3 minutes or until caramels begin to melt. Whisk until smooth. Stir in 1 cup of nuts.

6. Gently spread caramel mixture over brownie batter in pan. Sprinkle with chocolate chips.

7. Pour remaining unbaked brownie batter evenly over caramel mixture; sprinkle with remaining nuts.

8. Bake for an additional 30 minutes.

9. Cool in pan. Run a knife around edge of pan to loosen brownies from sides. Lift from pan using foil as handles. Cut into 24 brownies.

Made in the USA
Lexington, KY
26 November 2019